AF656279

Sanjeev Kapoor's

NO-OIL Recipes

In association with Alyona Kapoor

Popular Prakashan

www.popularprakashan.com

Published by
POPULAR PRAKASHAN PVT. LTD.
301, Mahalaxmi Chambers
22, Bhulabhai Desai Road
Mumbai - 400026
for KHANA KHAZANA PUBLICATIONS PVT. LTD.

First Published 2008
Fifth Reprint August 2014

(4157)
ISBN 978-81-7991-409-0

Photography: Mangesh Parab
Nutritionists: Prachi Hatwalne and Kirti Masurkar

PRINTED IN INDIA
by Saurabh Printers Pvt. Ltd.
A-16, Sector 4, Noida

Author's Note

Life is more fun and interesting if there is a challenge before you. This book was definitely interesting to write and of course challenging because my focus was totally on making oil-free food look great and taste good. And believe me, gone are the morose days when oil-free meant boiled steamed food with a dash of salt and pepper. It does not mean *khichdi* and *dahi* any more. Mealtimes are eminently more fulfilling if there is some access to recipes that you can enjoy along with the family given the fact that the food has to be oil-free.

A lot has been said and written about "low-oil" or "no-oil" diets, but how well the subject has been understood is the moot question. Modern life brings with it loads of stress, tension and related health problems. The progress in science has introduced various gadgets and means to relieve physical strain but then that very relief has given rise to ailments : though we have adjusted to the modern way of life we have not really been able to adjust our diet accordingly. I should say let us forget the journey but enjoy the final destination: in other words, my recipes are for everyday cooking. In this day and age when middle age diseases referred to so nonchalantly as "lifestyle diseases" are on the rise, I am sure some of you would welcome this new addition to the kitchen. There are recipes for all courses in a meal, and each of them has been totally researched and perfected.

Oil has always been an important constituent of most cuisines around the world for it not only adds taste, but also imparts its own flavour. For example, coconut oil, olive oil, mustard oil etc. But along with the flavours comes the high fat content and the dense calories which are restricted for some of us for medical reasons. As you go along the book you will see that we have tried not to use any oil or ghee or cream or even certain ingredients with a high fat content. But at the same time, great care has been taken to ensure that the taste factor has not been much affected.

These recipes are meant not only for weight-watchers, they are for you and me who are health-conscious, who want to look better, live better and longer! My mantra is to eat well but sensibly and follow a regular exercise regime. These recipes are suggestions to bring a change into the daily diet and by all means, use them whenever the need is to try out oil-free cooking.

Each active person is allowed 15 grams of visible fat a day. But the truth is that we end up having a lot more than the allowed quantity because most of us are unaware that all foods contain some percentage of fat. Be it wheat, pulses, vegetables, fruits, skimmed milk, cottage cheese, yogurt, cloves, cinnamon, sesame seeds and even the miniscule single mustard seed! So if we do eat a variety of foods each day, in a variety of menus, balancing the carbohydrate and protein intake, all invisible fat included in this way is just perfect for a healthy diet. My point here is that "no-oil" does not mean that the food is totally free of lipid content.

It is important to keep the taste buds pampered because they rule the roost! The contents of this book do just that. All the recipes are written to provide for four portions. The portion size has been set keeping in mind that they form part of a menu which will have other complementary dishes and will be shared by a group of people.

So just tie up your aprons and armed with non-stick cookware try out this wonderful array of dishes that will not only help you live a healthy life but will also win hearts along the way.

Happy Cooking!

Contents

Main-Course - Seafood, Chicken And Mutton

Accompaniments

Sweets

Annexure

INGREDIENTS

2 teaspoons tea leaves
16 fresh mint leaves
4 lemons, cut into wedges
2 inches cinnamon
4 star anise (*chakri phool*)
16 teaspoons castor sugar

Moroccan Mint *Tea*

1. Place tea leaves, mint leaves, lemon wedges, cinnamon, star anise and castor sugar in a teapot.
2. Pour boiling water, cover the teapot and allow to infuse for about three to four minutes.
3. Stir well to dissolve the sugar.
4. Pour into individual glasses and serve hot.

Banana *and Honey Smoothie*

INGREDIENTS

5 medium ripe bananas, roughly chopped

5 tablespoons honey

2 tablespoons lemon juice

2 cups drained skimmed milk yogurt

10 ice cubes

10 fresh mint leaves, torn

1 Place roughly chopped bananas in a freezer for one hour.

2 Place the frozen banana pieces, honey, lemon juice and yogurt in a blender and blend until smooth.

3 Add ice cubes and blend again.

4 Pour into individual glasses and serve garnished with mint leaves.

INGREDIENTS

30 spinach leaves, finely chopped

3 medium potatoes, boiled and mashed

1 medium onion, finely chopped

4 cups Vegetable Stock (*page 92*)

Salt to taste

½ teaspoon black pepper powder

½ cup skimmed milk

Caldo Verde - *Spinach and Potato Soup*

1 Heat a deep non-stick pan. Add onion and cook for a couple of minutes taking care that the colour of the onion does not change.

2 Add vegetable stock and bring to a boil.

3 Add mashed potatoes and stir well to mix. Add spinach and cook till the leaves soften. Add salt to taste and black pepper powder.

4 Stir in the milk and bring to a boil and cook for a minute or two more.

5 Serve piping hot.

Hot and Sour *Chicken Soup*

INGREDIENTS

¼ cup chicken, boiled and chopped

1 slice bamboo shoot

3 tablespoons cornflour

1 small onion, chopped

2-3 garlic cloves, chopped

1 inch ginger, grated

2 inch celery stalk, chopped

½ medium carrot, grated

1 small piece cabbage, chopped

2 fresh button mushrooms, chopped

½ medium green capsicum, seeded and chopped

2 French beans, chopped

½ teaspoon white pepper powder

Salt to taste

½ teaspoon sugar

½ teaspoon MSG (optional)

2 tablespoons soy sauce

2 tablespoons green chilli sauce

1 Boil the bamboo shoot in one cup of water for two to three minutes, drain, cool and chop finely.

2 Mix cornflour and half a cup of water.

3 Heat a non-stick wok or a saucepan, add onion, garlic, ginger and cook for a few seconds. Add celery, carrot, cabbage, bamboo shoot, mushroom, capsicum and French beans.

4 Cook for two to three minutes or until vegetables are almost cooked, stirring continuously. Add chicken and cook for one minute more.

5 Add white pepper powder, salt to taste, sugar, MSG, soy sauce, green chilli sauce and mix well.

4-5 cups Chicken Stock (*page 92*)

2 tablespoons vinegar

1 stalk spring onion greens, chopped

Chef's Tip: *We have used tinned bamboo shoot slices, which are preserved in brine, hence they should be boiled in water for two to three minutes before use.*

6 Stir in chicken stock and bring to a boil. Stir in cornflour mixture and continue to cook for a minute or until the soup thickens.

7 Stir in vinegar and serve piping hot, garnished with spring onion greens.

Tropical Chicken *and Farfalle Salad*

INGREDIENTS

- 200 grams boneless chicken, boiled and shredded
- 1 cup farfalle (bow-tie pasta)
- 1 medium tomato, cut into ½-inch cubes
- 1 medium carrot, cut into ½-inch cubes
- ½ medium green capsicum, seeded, cut into ½-inch cubes
- ½ medium yellow capsicum, seeded, cut into ½-inch cubes (optional)
- 8-10 olives, cut into rings

FOR THE DRESSING

- 4-5 garlic cloves, chopped
- 2 inch celery stalk, finely chopped
- ½ teaspoon crushed red chillies
- 2-3 tablespoons lemon juice
- Salt to taste
- 2 teaspoons finely chopped fresh parsley

1. Boil three cups of water in a deep pan. Add pasta and cook till just done. Drain and set aside to cool.

2. To make the dressing, combine garlic, celery, red chillies, lemon juice, salt and parsley. Mix well.

3. In a bowl, mix together pasta, chicken, tomato, carrot, green capsicum, yellow capsicum and olives. Pour the prepared dressing over and toss to mix. Serve immediately.

INGREDIENTS

400 grams fresh button mushrooms, quartered

Salt to taste

2 teaspoons garlic paste

5-6 fresh basil leaves

5 tablespoons sugar

2 teaspoons balsamic vinegar

7-8 black peppercorns, crushed

Mushrooms in Balsamic Vinegar

1 Marinate mushrooms in a mixture of salt, garlic paste and roughly torn basil leaves for two hours.

2 Heat sugar in a pan. Add one tablespoon of water, stir continuously till it caramelises to a light golden colour.

3 Add balsamic vinegar and crushed peppercorns and cook for three to four minutes.

4 Toss mushrooms in caramelised sugar mixture and refrigerate.

5 Serve chilled.

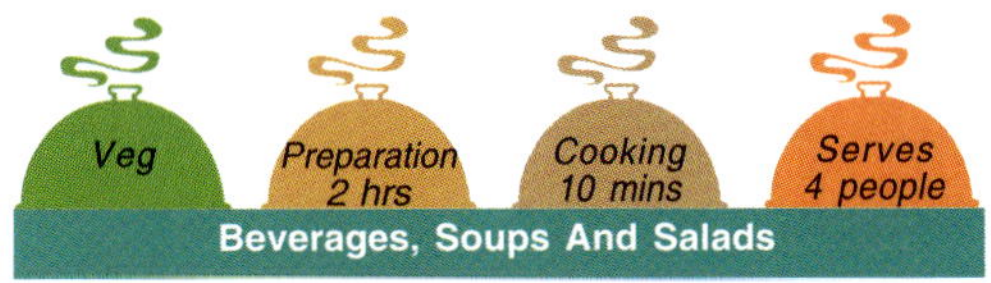

Vegetable *Tacos*

INGREDIENTS

FOR THE TACOS

¼ cup maize flour (*makai ka atta*)

4 teaspoons refined flour (*maida*)

A small pinch of turmeric powder

Salt to taste

FOR THE FILLING

2 medium potatoes, peeled and quartered

½ cup green peas, shelled

5-6 French beans, strings removed

1 medium carrot, cut into four pieces

¼ teaspoon turmeric powder

Salt to taste

1 large onion, finely chopped

1. Mix all the ingredients for the tacos, add sufficient water and knead into a medium soft dough. Keep covered with a damp cloth for about fifteen minutes.
2. Divide into sixteen equal portions and roll into thin *puris*. Prick the *puris* with a fork.
3. Heat a non-stick *tawa*. Dry roast the *puris* on both sides. Fold over a rolling pin while still hot into a half-moon shape. Set aside to cool.
4. Boil potatoes, peas, French beans and carrot in sufficient water with turmeric powder and salt till done. When cooked, drain, mash and set aside to cool.
5. Heat a non-stick pan. Roast onion for two minutes. Add garlic and roast for another minute.
6. Add red chilli paste, salt and tomato ketchup. Cook for two minutes.

3-4 garlic cloves, finely chopped

1 teaspoon red chilli paste

2 tablespoons tomato ketchup

½ cup bean sprouts

1 head of lettuce, shredded

7 Add mashed vegetables and cook for another five to eight minutes. Take off the heat and cool.

8 To serve, stuff taco shells with the prepared filling. Top with bean sprouts and lettuce leaves. Serve immediately.

Veg | Preparation 15mins | Cooking 30 mins | Serves 4 people

Roasted Garlic *Prawns*

INGREDIENTS

200 grams prawns, peeled and deveined

1 teaspoon garlic paste

½ medium carrot

Salt to taste

7-8 black peppercorns, crushed

1 teaspoon lemon juice

2 teaspoons mustard paste

2 tablespoons tomato ketchup

10-15 garlic cloves, chopped

6-8 small onions, peeled

8 small broccoli florets

3-4 fresh basil leaves

1 Peel, wash and cut carrot into half-inch pieces. Put in sufficient boiling water and cook till nearly done. Drain and set aside.

2 Mix together garlic paste, salt, crushed peppercorns, lemon juice, mustard paste, tomato ketchup and garlic. Marinate prawns along with small onions, carrot and broccoli in this mixture for half an hour.

3 Heat a non-stick pan. Place marinated prawns and vegetables in it and cook for three to four minutes or till done. Alternatively, grill in a combi-microwave oven for three to four minutes.

4 Serve hot, garnished with roughly torn fresh basil leaves.

Non-Veg | Preparation 10 mins | Cooking 5 mins | Serves 4 people

Chicken *Olivetti*

INGREDIENTS

4 (200 grams each) boneless chicken breasts

2 teaspoons ginger paste

2 teaspoons garlic paste

½ teaspoon black pepper powder

1 teaspoon soy sauce

Salt to taste

2 tablespoons lemon juice

½ teaspoon red chilli flakes

½ teaspoon mixed herbs

12-16 green olives, stoned

2 medium tomatoes, cut into 1½-inch pieces

7-8 black peppercorns, crushed

2-3 fresh parsley sprigs

1 Cut each chicken breast into one-inch wide strips.

2 In a bowl, mix ginger paste, garlic paste, pepper powder, soy sauce and salt. Add lemon juice and marinate the chicken pieces in this mixture. Add red chilli flakes and mixed herbs and mix again. Rest for half an hour in a refrigerator.

3 Wrap a chicken strip around each olive and secure it with a toothpick. Reserve marinade.

4 Heat a non-stick pan and place the chicken olivettis on it. Cook, tossing the pieces occasionally, till chicken is almost done.

5 Add tomatoes mixed with reserved marinade. Stir and cook till the chicken is done. Add crushed black peppercorns and toss. Arrange chicken olivettis on a plate and garnish with fresh parsley sprigs. Serve hot.

Rice *Panki*

INGREDIENTS

½ cup rice flour, sifted

8 tablespoons skimmed milk yogurt, whisked

Salt to taste

1 teaspoon green chilli paste

½ teaspoon ginger paste

½ teaspoon soda bicarbonate

3 banana leaves, cut into 5-inch squares or circles

FOR THE STUFFING

½ cup sprouted green gram (*ankurit moong*)

Salt to taste

3-4 black peppercorns, crushed

¼ teaspoon red chilli flakes

1 Place the rice flour in a bowl. Add yogurt and salt and mix well. Add green chilli paste and ginger paste and mix again. Add enough water to make a batter of pouring consistency. Add soda bicarbonate and mix. Cover and set aside to ferment for about two hours.

2 Mix all the ingredients for the stuffing together.

3 Heat a non-stick *tawa*.

4 Pour rice batter on each banana leaf, place the stuffing in the centre and fold the leaf into half. Place it on the *tawa* and cook for two to three minutes. Turn and cook the other side as well.

5 Serve the *panki* in the banana leaf.

Veg

Preparation 2 hrs

Cooking 15 mins

Serves 4 people

INGREDIENTS

6 medium potatoes

1 medium onion, finely chopped

Salt to taste

7-8 black peppercorns, ground coarsely

A pinch of nutmeg powder

2 tablespoons fresh parsley, chopped

Hash Brown Potatoes

1 Boil potatoes in sufficient water till nearly done. They should be slightly undercooked. Peel and grate potatoes. Heat a non-stick pan. Add onion and roast till translucent. Remove from heat. Preheat oven to 200°C/400°F/Gas Mark 6.

2 Mix grated potatoes and roasted onion along with salt, half the ground peppercorns and nutmeg powder. Mix well and put in a baking tray and spread evenly with your fingers.

3 Sprinkle the remaining ground peppercorns over the potatoes. Bake in the preheated oven for ten to fifteen minutes or till the potatoes turn light brown.

4 Cut into wedges, garnish with parsley and serve hot.

Veg

Preparation 15 mins

Cooking 15 mins

Serves 4 people

INGREDIENTS

- 4 (200 grams each) boneless chicken breasts, cut into 1-inch pieces
- 5-6 whole dried red chillies, seeded
- 2 medium onions
- 8-10 garlic cloves
- 2-3 fresh parsley sprigs
- 7-8 fresh basil leaves
- ½ tablespoon lemon juice
- 1 tablespoon Worcestershire sauce

Caribbean Chicken *Kebabs*

1. Chop one onion and cut the other into one-inch square pieces.
2. Make a coarse paste of whole red chillies, chopped onion, garlic, parsley, basil, lemon juice, Worcestershire sauce, peppercorns, curry powder and salt. Transfer the paste into a bowl and add the chicken pieces. Mix well.
3. Add capsicum, pineapple, tomato and onion and marinate for two hours preferably in a refrigerator.
4. Thread chicken, capsicum, pineapple, tomato and onion pieces one after the other onto skewers. Reserve the remaining marinade for basting.

5-6 black peppercorns

½ teaspoon curry powder

Salt to taste

1 medium green capsicum, seeded, cut into 1-inch pieces

2 slices canned pineapple, cut into 1-inch pieces

1 medium tomato, seeded, cut into 1-inch pieces

5 Heat a non-stick *tawa*. Place the skewers on the *tawa* and cook, basting with the reserved marinade half way through, for ten to twelve minutes or until chicken is done, rotating the skewers continuously.

6 Serve hot.

INGREDIENTS

1 cup soya granules

2½ cups skimmed milk

4-5 medium potatoes, boiled and mashed

1 medium onion, finely chopped

2 green chillies, finely chopped

2 tablespoons fresh coriander leaves, finely chopped

¼ teaspoon cumin powder

1 teaspoon red chilli powder

¼ teaspoon clove powder

¼ teaspoon cinnamon powder

Soya *Burgers*

1 Soak soya granules in two cups of milk for fifteen minutes. Drain and squeeze out excess milk. Grind to mince the granules further.

2 In a large mixing bowl, mix together soya granules, mashed potatoes, onion, green chillies, coriander leaves, cumin powder, red chilli powder, clove powder, cinnamon powder, lemon juice and salt.

3 Divide the mixture into four equal portions. Shape each portion into a patty of three inches diameter and about half an inch thick.

4 Coat each patty evenly with breadcrumbs.

5 Heat a non-stick pan and cook the patties on both sides till crisp.

1½ teaspoons lemon juice

Salt to taste

¾ cup brown breadcrumbs

TO SERVE

4 burger buns

4 tablespoons mustard paste

4 tablespoons tomato ketchup

10-12 lettuce leaves

1 medium onion, sliced into rings

6 Halve a burger bun horizontally. Apply mustard paste on the lower half and tomato ketchup on the top half. Place two or three lettuce leaves on the lower half. Place the patty on it, top with onion rings, cover with the top half of the bun and serve immediately.

INGREDIENTS

3 large bunches (600 grams each) spinach, chopped

10-12 baby corn cobs, cut into ½-inch pieces

2 medium onions, cut into 1-inch pieces

5-6 garlic cloves, chopped

2-3 green chillies, slit

1 medium green capsicum, seeded and cut into 1-inch pieces

2 tablespoons cornflour

¾ cup Vegetable Stock (*page 92*)

Salt to taste

¼ teaspoon MSG (optional)

¼ teaspoon black pepper powder

Palak Baby Corn Sabzi

1. Blanch the baby corn in two cups of boiling water for two to three minutes. Drain and set aside.

2. Heat a non-stick pan. Add onions and garlic and cook for two minutes.

3. Add green chillies, capsicum and baby corn and cook on high heat for two to three minutes.

4. Add spinach and toss. Add cornflour mixed with the vegetable stock and cook, stirring, for two to three minutes.

5. Stir in salt, MSG and pepper powder and serve hot.

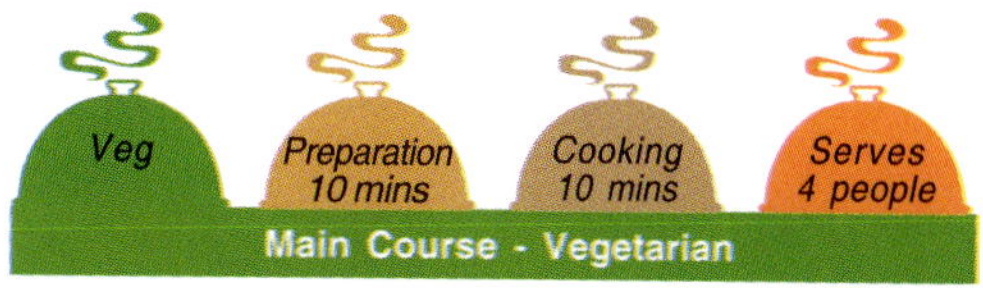

Tabbouleh-Stuffed Tomatoes

INGREDIENTS

- ½ cup cracked wheat (burghul)
- 8 medium firm red tomatoes
- 2-3 spring onions, chopped
- 1 small radish, grated
- 2 tablespoons raisins (*kishmish*)
- 2 tablespoons lemon juice
- Salt to taste
- 5-6 black peppercorns, crushed
- 3 tablespoons fresh parsley, chopped
- 6-8 lettuce leaves
- 6-8 fresh mint leaves

1. Soak the burghul in boiling water for half an hour. Drain, squeeze out excess water and set aside.

2. Cut off the tops of the tomatoes and scoop out the seeds. Reserve the seeds.

3. Mix together burghul, spring onions, radish, raisins, lemon juice, salt, crushed peppercorns, parsley and reserved tomato seeds. Stuff the tomatoes with this filling.

4. Heat sufficient water in a steamer. Place stuffed tomatoes on a perforated plate in the steamer and steam for ten minutes. Remove and set aside to cool for a while. Serve warm, on a bed of lettuce, garnished with roughly torn mint leaves.

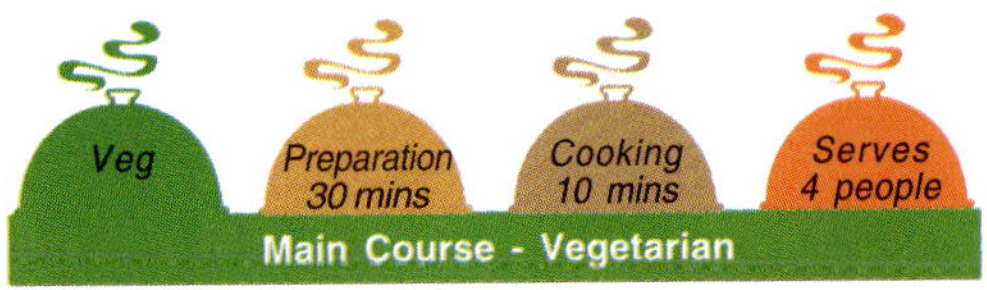

INGREDIENTS

- 2 large bunches (600 grams each) spinach
- 4 medium potatoes
- 4 medium onions
- 8-10 garlic cloves, chopped
- Salt to taste
- 7-8 black peppercorns, crushed
- ½ teaspoon Tabasco sauce
- ¾ cup skimmed milk
- A pinch of nutmeg powder
- ½ cup brown breadcrumbs

Spinach and Potato Bake

1. Blanch spinach in sufficient boiling water for one minute. Drain, refresh in cold water and chop.

2. Boil two potatoes, peel and mash till smooth. Peel and slice the remaining two potatoes into thin slices. Blanch in hot water for two to three minutes, drain and set aside. Chop two onions and slice the remaining two into rings.

3. Preheat the oven to 180°C/350°F/Gas Mark 4.

4. Heat a non-stick pan and roast chopped onions and garlic till light brown. Add spinach (first press it with your hands to remove excess water). Cook for a few minutes till all the water is absorbed. Add salt, half the crushed peppercorns and Tabasco sauce. Set aside.

5 Heat another non-stick pan. Toss the potato slices and onion rings together. Add salt and remaining crushed peppercorns and toss again.

6 Mix the mashed potatoes, milk and nutmeg powder together to a smooth mixture. Transfer into a piping bag with a star nozzle.

7 Take an ovenproof dish and layer the spinach mixture and potato and onion mixture alternately. Sprinkle the breadcrumbs over the last layer. Pipe mashed potato rosettes on top and bake for thirty minutes.

8 Serve hot.

INGREDIENTS

1 medium carrot, cut into diamonds

½ small cauliflower, separated into small florets

2-3 baby brinjals

1 medium potato, cut into ½-inch cubes

5 stalks lemon grass

1 teaspoon lemon juice

Salt to taste

¾ cup fresh coconut milk

2-3 fresh basil leaves

GREEN CURRY PASTE

10 green chillies

3 shallots (*sambhar* onions)

9 garlic cloves

1 inch galangal

Thai Green Curry with Vegetables

1. To make green curry paste, grind green chillies, shallots, garlic, galangal, lemon grass, lemon rind, coriander roots, coriander seeds, cumin seeds and salt to a fine paste.

2. Blanch all the vegetables individually in boiling water and refresh in cold water. Tie lemon grass in a muslin to make a bundle. Crush it slightly.

3. Heat a non-stick pan, add green curry paste and roast for one minute. Add the blanched vegetables and lemon juice and cook for three to four minutes, stirring continuously.

4. Add three cups of water and continue to cook. Add lemon grass bundle and cook for three to four minutes till the curry absorbs its flavour.

3 inch stalk lemon grass

¼ teaspoon lemon rind, grated

A small bunch of coriander roots

2 teaspoons coriander seeds

2 teaspoons cumin seeds

Salt to taste

Chef s Tip: *Galangal is a type of ginger used in Thai cooking. If not available, use ginger.*

5 Remove the lemon grass and add salt and coconut milk. Simmer for one minute.

6 Add basil leaves and take off the heat. Serve hot.

Middle Eastern Vegetable Stew

INGREDIENTS

2 medium potatoes, peeled, cut into 1-inch cubes

2 medium carrots, peeled, cut into 1-inch cubes

1 green capsicum, seeded, cut into 1-inch pieces

2 medium zucchini, cut into 1-inch pieces

1 small bunch spinach, chopped

½ cup chickpeas (*Kabuli chana*)

3 cups Vegetable Stock (*page 92*)

1 inch ginger, sliced

3-4 cloves

8-10 black peppercorns

1. Wash and soak chickpeas in sufficient water overnight or for at least six hours. Pressure cook till done and set aside.

2. Heat vegetable stock in a saucepan and bring to a boil.

3. Tie ginger slices, cloves and peppercorns in a muslin and add to the boiling stock.

4. Add boiled chickpeas, potatoes, carrots, celery, cumin powder and red chilli powder. Mix well and cook on medium heat till it begins to boil.

1 celery stalk, cut into 1 inch pieces

1 teaspoon cumin powder

A pinch of red chilli powder

Salt to taste

½ teaspoon black pepper powder

10 fresh mint leaves

5 Cover and simmer on low heat till all the vegetables are cooked and tender. Add the capsicum, zucchini and spinach and cook for two minutes. Remove the spice bundle and discard.

6 Season with salt and pepper powder and garnish with mint leaves. Serve hot.

Veg | Preparation 15 mins | Cooking 30 mins | Serves 4 people

Chilli-Garlic *Prawns*

INGREDIENTS

16-20 medium prawns (400 grams), peeled and deveined

3 medium tomatoes, chopped

Salt to taste

1 inch ginger, cut into thin strips

2 tablespoons fresh coriander leaves, chopped

FOR THE SPICE PASTE

1 inch ginger, coarsely chopped

10-12 garlic cloves, coarsely chopped

6-8 whole dried red chillies, seeded

¼ teaspoon turmeric powder

1½ teaspoons cumin seeds

1. Grind the ginger, garlic, red chilies, turmeric powder and cumin seeds to a fine paste.
2. Heat a non-stick pan. Add tomatoes, ground spice paste and salt and cook for three to four minutes on moderate heat till the paste is almost dry.
3. Add prawns and cook till done.
4. Serve hot, garnished with ginger strips and coriander leaves.

INGREDIENTS

1 cup small prawns, peeled and deveined

1 small tender coconut (*daab*)

2 medium onions, finely sliced

4-5 green chillies, slit

¼ cup scraped coconut

1 teaspoon ginger paste

1½ teaspoons garlic paste

Salt to taste

¼ teaspoon turmeric powder

¼ cup tender coconut flesh (*malai*), chopped

½ teaspoon *panch phoron*

Wholewheat flour (*atta*) dough, as required

Daab *Chingri*

1. Take a tender coconut (*daab*), cut off a slice from the top, drain the water and scoop out the flesh; retain the top to use as a lid.
2. Wash prawns thoroughly under running water. Drain completely.
3. Preheat the oven to 220°C/425°F/Gas Mark 7.
4. In a bowl, mix prawns, onions, green chillies, coconut, ginger paste, garlic paste, salt, turmeric powder and tender coconut flesh.
5. Heat a non-stick pan. Add *panch phoron* and when the seeds crackle, add to the mixture.
6. Fill the *daab* with the mixture.

Note: *Panch phoron is a mixture of equal quantities of five spices : mustard seeds, fenugreek seeds, fennel seeds, cumin seeds and onion seeds. It is used extensively in Bengali cooking.*

7 Cover the *daab* using the reserved top slice. Seal the top with *atta* dough.

8 Bake for approximately thirty minutes. Let it stand for ten more minutes. Open the seal just before serving.

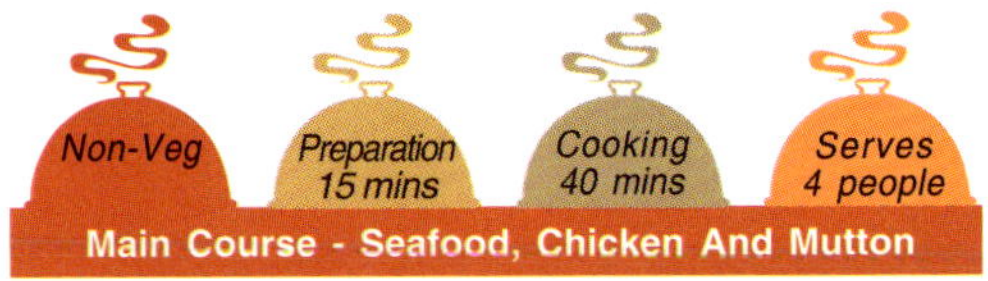

Goan Fish Curry

INGREDIENTS

- 2 pomfrets (400 grams each) or any flat fish
- 1 small onion, chopped
- 2 green chillies, slit and halved
- Salt to taste
- 1 tablespoon malt vinegar

FOR THE SPICE PASTE

- 2 teaspoons cumin seeds
- 2 tablespoons coriander seeds
- 6 whole dried red chillies
- ½ cup scraped coconut
- 2 inches ginger coarsely chopped
- 15 cloves garlic, coarsely chopped
- 1 tablespoon tamarind pulp

1. Cut each pomfret into six slices. Dry roast cumin seeds, coriander seeds and whole red chillies.

2. Make a fine paste of all the roasted spices along with coconut, ginger, garlic and tamarind with a little water. Apply half the ground paste to the fish.

3. Heat a non-stick pan. Add onions and roast till light brown. Add green chillies. Cook on medium heat for three minutes, stirring constantly.

4. Add the remaining ground paste and stir well. Cook for three minutes, on low heat, till it emits a pleasant aroma. Add one and a half cups of water and bring to a boil. Add the marinated fish and salt. Cook on low heat for about five minutes or till fish is just done. Stir in vinegar and serve hot with steamed rice.

Grilled Fish *in Salsa*

INGREDIENTS

8 King fish (*surmai*) darnes
Salt to taste
3 tablespoons lemon juice
2 tablespoons malt vinegar
2 tablespoons English mustard paste
1 tablespoon ginger-garlic paste
1 tablespoon red chilli sauce
16 cloves

FOR THE SALSA

½ cup corn kernels
10-12 fresh basil leaves
1 large onion, roasted and chopped
4-5 garlic cloves, roasted and finely chopped
2 medium tomatoes, chopped

1 Marinate fish darnes in salt, lemon juice, malt vinegar, English mustard paste, ginger-garlic paste and red chilli sauce for half an hour.

2 Preheat the grill.

3 Stud marinated darnes with cloves, place them under the hot grill and cook for eight to ten minutes (or until fish flakes easily with a fork) turning once. Do not overcook the fish. Remove cloves.

4 To make the salsa, boil corn kernels with one cup of water for two to three minutes; drain. You can also cook them on Microwave HIGH (100%) for one minute.

5 Tear basil leaves roughly, reserving a few to garnish. Mix together corn, onion, garlic, tomatoes, pineapple, jalapeno pepper, salt, basil leaves, lemon juice and coriander leaves.

2 canned pineapple slices, chopped

1 jalapeno pepper, finely chopped

Salt to taste

1 tablespoon lemon juice

2 tablespoons fresh coriander leaves, finely chopped

Note: *Darnes are thick slices of fish cut on the bone.*

Chef s Tip: *Jalapeno peppers belong to the capsicum family. These peppers are very pungent and are used extensively in Mexican cooking.*

6 To serve, spread salsa on a plate. Place grilled fish on it and garnish with reserved basil leaves.

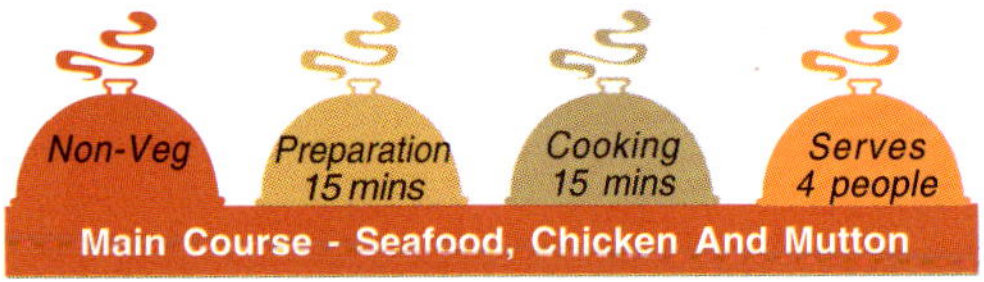

Fish *in* Tomato Pepper Sauce

INGREDIENTS

1 King fish (*surmai*) (600-700 grams)

2 tablespoons lemon juice

½ teaspoon dried oregano

1 teaspoon dried basil

Salt to taste

15-16 black peppercorns, crushed

2-3 garlic cloves, chopped

FOR THE SAUCE

6 garlic cloves, chopped

1 medium onion, chopped

2 cups Tomato Concasse (see below)

½ cup white wine (optional)

3 tablespoons tomato ketchup

Note: *For Tomato Concasse, blanch tomatoes in sufficient boiling water for two minutes. Drain, refresh in cold water, peel, cut, remove seeds and chop.*

1 Fillet the fish and cut into four steaks. Combine lemon juice, half the oregano, basil, salt, peppercorns and garlic and smear the fish steaks with the paste. Set aside to marinate for twenty to thirty minutes.

2 In a non-stick frying pan, roast garlic and onion till brown. Add tomato concasse, remaining oregano, white wine and tomato ketchup and cook for a couple of minutes.

3 Add marinated fish steaks. Cover and cook till done. Serve hot.

Burghul-Crusted Chicken

INGREDIENTS

4 boneless chicken breasts with skin (200 grams each)

1½ cup cracked wheat (burghul)

2 egg whites

¼ tablespoon wholewheat flour (*atta*)

Salt to taste

3-4 black peppercorns, crushed

FOR THE MARINADE

2 medium onions, chopped

10 garlic cloves, chopped

1 celery stalk, chopped

½ teaspoon red chilli powder

2 tablespoons soy sauce

1 Boil five cups of water. Take off the heat and add burghul. After half a minute drain the burghul and tie up in a muslin to drain. When completely dry empty onto a plate.

2 To make the marinade, combine onions, garlic, celery, red chilli powder, soy sauce, vinegar, salt and crushed peppercorns. Add chicken breasts and marinate for an hour, preferably in the refrigerator.

3 Preheat oven to 200°C/400°F/Gas Mark 6.

4 Whisk egg whites, wholewheat flour, salt and crushed peppercorns together to make a smooth batter.

5 Dip chicken breasts in the batter, then roll them in burghul. Press lightly.

1 tablespoon vinegar

Salt to taste

3-4 black peppercorns, crushed

FOR THE SAUCE

4 medium tomatoes, blanched and puréed

8 garlic cloves, chopped

2 medium onions, chopped

4 tablespoons tomato ketchup

Salt to taste

3-4 black peppercorns, crushed

½ teaspoon dried oregano

6 Heat a non-stick pan and place the chicken breasts on it. Cook on high heat for half a minute on each side to seal the juices. Transfer to a baking tray and bake for ten minutes or till done.

7 To make the sauce, blanch tomatoes in sufficient boiling water for two minutes. Drain, peel and purée.

8 Heat another non-stick pan. Add garlic and onions and cook till the onion turn translucent. Add tomato purée and tomato ketchup and bring the mixture to a boil.

9 Add one and one-fourth cups of water and cook for eight to ten minutes till it reaches the consistency of a sauce. Add salt, crushed peppercorns, and oregano and stir to mix.

10 Place chicken breasts on a serving plate, pour the sauce over and serve hot.

Non-Veg | Preparation 20 mins | Cooking 30 mins | Serves 4 people

INGREDIENTS

4 fillets of pomfret (400 grams)

Salt to taste

4 tablespoons lemon juice

1 cup fresh coriander leaves

4 green chillies

½ cup scraped coconut

3 teaspoons cumin seeds

6-8 garlic cloves

3-4 banana leaves

Fish in *Banana Leaves*

1 Clean, wash and cut fish fillets into two-inch by one-and-a-half-inch pieces. Sprinkle salt and half of the lemon juice and set aside for half an hour.

2 Grind coriander leaves, green chillies, coconut, cumin seeds and garlic to a fine paste. Add salt and remaining lemon juice to it. Mix well.

3 Apply this marinade to fish fillets and marinate for at least fifteen minutes. Cut banana leaves into four pieces each.

4 Put one marinated piece of fish on each piece of banana leaf along with a little of the marinade and fold the leaves to seal tightly. Steam the fish in a steamer for fifteen minutes and serve hot.

Non-Veg | Preparation 30 mins | Cooking 15 mins | Serves 4 people

Main Course - Seafood, Chicken And Mutton

Chicken *Stew*

INGREDIENTS

800 grams chicken on the bone, cut into 1½-inch pieces

7-8 garlic cloves, sliced

2 medium onions, sliced

2 medium carrots, cut into 1-inch cubes

2 medium potatoes, cut into 1-inch cubes

2 tablespoons wholewheat flour (*atta*)

Salt to taste

5 cups Chicken Stock (*page 92*)

¼ teaspoon black pepper powder

6-8 French beans, cut into 1-inch pieces

½ cup skimmed milk

1 Heat a non-stick pan and add garlic, onions, carrots and potatoes and roast for four to five minutes on high heat.

2 Add wholewheat flour to the vegetables and roast for a minute. Add chicken pieces and salt and cook for three to four minutes. Add stock and bring to a boil. Add half the pepper powder. Cover and cook for three to four minutes.

3 Uncover, add French beans, mix and cook for a minute. Add the milk and the remaining pepper powder. Cover and cook on medium heat for seven to eight minutes.

4 Serve hot.

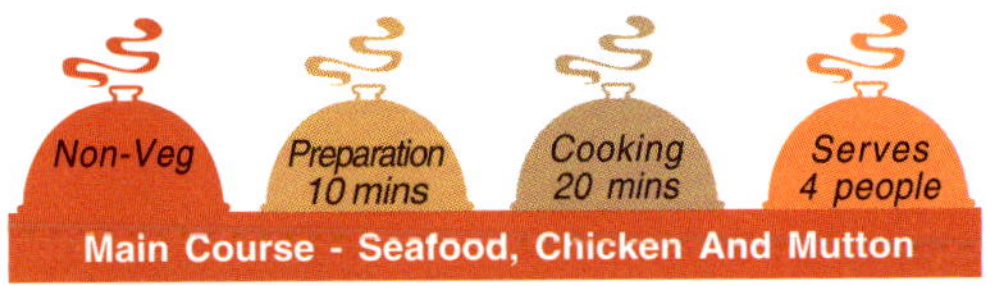

INGREDIENTS

1 whole chicken (800 grams), 8 pieces on the bone

¼ small bunch fresh fenugreek leaves (*methi*), chopped

1 cup skimmed milk yogurt, whisked

Salt to taste

4 one-inch pieces of ginger

5 green cardamoms

1 black cardamom

5 cloves

1 inch cinnamon

1 bay leaf

1-2 blades mace (*javitri*)

2 large onions, chopped

20 garlic cloves, chopped

3 green chillies, seeded and chopped

Methi *Murgh*

1 Mix together yogurt and salt in a large bowl. Add chicken and marinate for about half an hour. Chop half the ginger and cut the rest into thin strips.

2 Heat a non-stick pan, add green cardamoms, black cardamom, cloves, cinnamon, bay leaf and mace and roast over medium heat till fragrant.

3 Add onions and cook till they turn golden brown. Add garlic, chopped ginger and green chillies and cook for two minutes.

4 Add turmeric powder, coriander powder, red chilli powder and one-fourth cup of water. Stir and cook for half a minute.

5 Add tomatoes and cook till soft.

½ teaspoon turmeric powder

1 teaspoon coriander power

1 teaspoon red chilli powder

2 medium tomatoes, chopped

1 tablespoon dried fenugreek leaves *(kasoori methi)*

¼ cup fresh coriander leaves, chopped

6 Add marinated chicken, fenugreek leaves and mix well. Cover and simmer till chicken is almost done. Adjust seasoning.

7 Sprinkle *kasoori methi*, ginger strips and coriander leaves. Remove from heat and keep covered for five minutes before serving.

Non-Veg | Preparation 30 mins | Cooking 20 mins | Serves 4 people

Sweet and Sour Chicken

INGREDIENTS

400 grams boneless chicken, cut into 1-inch pieces

Salt to taste

3 tablespoons cornflour

3 cups Chicken Stock (*page 92*)

4 tablespoons tomato sauce

2 tablespoons sugar

½ cup pineapple juice

¼ teaspoon MSG (optional)

½ teaspoon white pepper powder

1 medium green capsicum, seeded

½ medium red capsicum, seeded

½ medium yellow capsicum, seeded

1 pineapple slice

1 inch ginger, finely chopped

4-6 garlic cloves, finely chopped

1 medium onion, quartered and layers separated

2 tablespoons vinegar

1 Apply salt to the chicken pieces and set aside for fifteen minutes. Mix cornflour and one cup of chicken stock.

2 Mix tomato sauce, sugar, pineapple juice, MSG, white pepper powder and salt with one cup of chicken stock. Cut the green, red and yellow capsicums and pineapple into one-inch pieces. Heat a non-stick pan, add ginger and garlic and cook for one minute.

3 Add onion and continue to cook for a minute more. Stir in sauce and spice mix, green, red and yellow capsicums, remaining stock and chicken pieces. Cook for four to five minutes. Add the cornflour mixture and cook till the sauce starts to thicken, stirring continuously. Add pineapple pieces and vinegar. Mix and take off the heat. Serve hot.

Spicy *Salsa Chicken*

INGREDIENTS

2 boneless chicken breasts, (200 grams each), cut into 1-inch pieces

FOR THE SALSA

Concasse of 5 medium tomatoes (*page 45*)

1 medium onion, chopped

4 garlic cloves, chopped

2-3 jalapeno chillies, chopped

½ teaspoon oregano

Salt to taste

7-8 black peppercorns, crushed

1 tablespoon lemon juice

1 teaspoon fresh parsley, chopped

6 olives, stoned and chopped

2 tablespoons fresh coriander leaves, chopped

1 lemon, sliced

1 Mix tomato concasse, onion, garlic, jalapenos, oregano, salt, peppercorns, lemon juice, parsley and olives together.

2 Marinate chicken cubes in this mixture for about fifteen minutes.

3 Heat a deep non-stick pan and cook the marinated chicken cubes till done, stirring occasionally.

4 Serve hot, garnished with coriander leaves and lemon slices.

Chicken and Rice *Bake*

INGREDIENTS

2 cups chicken mince
1 cup Basmati rice
1 teaspoon dried thyme
4-6 black peppercorns
Salt to taste
2 bay leaves
2 medium onions, halved
4 medium tomatoes, halved
10-12 garlic cloves, chopped
20 black peppercorns, crushed
3-4 leaves fresh basil

1. Soak rice in three cups of water for half an hour. Drain and set aside.

2. Boil three cups of water in a deep pan, add thyme, black peppercorns, salt and bay leaves. Add soaked rice and cook till the rice is three-fourth done. Drain excess water and set aside.

3. Place onions and tomatoes along with garlic on a baking tray and cook in the oven till charred. Cool and chop roughly.

4. Heat a non-stick pan, add the chicken mince and keep stirring till the juices have completely evaporated.

5. Add roasted onions, tomatoes and garlic along with salt and crushed black peppercorns and mix well. Cover the pan and cook for a minute.

1½ cups Tomato Concasse (*page 45*)

3 tablespoons fresh brown breadcrumbs

1 teaspoon fresh parsley, chopped

6 Once the mince is cooked, tear basil leaves with your fingers and add to the mince. Mix well.

7 Preheat the oven to 200°C/400°F/Gas Mark 6.

8 In a casserole or baking dish, arrange layers of half the tomato concasse, half the rice and half the chicken. Repeat the layers. Finally top with fresh breadcrumbs and bake for fifteen minutes.

9 Take out of the oven when breadcrumbs are a light golden brown.

10 Garnish with parsley and serve immediately.

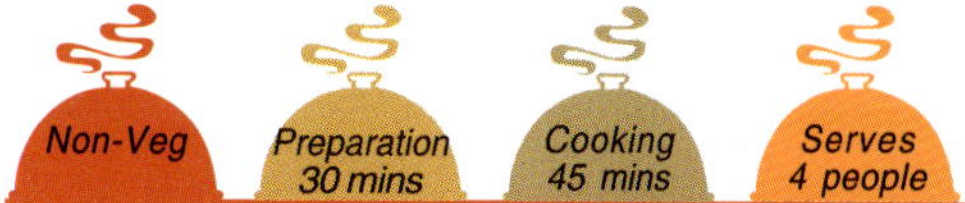

Honey and Orange Glazed Chicken

INGREDIENTS

4 tablespoons honey

6 tablespoons orange juice

4 boneless chicken breasts, (200 grams each)

1 inch ginger, chopped

Salt to taste

2 tablespoons mustard paste

3-4 black peppercorns, crushed

1 teaspoon red chilli flakes

2 tablespoons lemon juice

8-10 baby onions, peeled

2 medium carrots, thickly sliced

FOR THE GLAZE

2 tablespoons honey

1 cup orange juice

½ teaspoon red chilli flakes

2 teaspoons mustard paste

1 In a bowl, mix ginger, salt, mustard paste, orange juice, crushed black peppercorns, red chilli flakes, honey and lemon juice. Marinate the chicken in this mixture for about an hour. Preheat the oven to 200°C/400°F/ Gas Mark 6. Heat a non-stick pan. Add baby onions and carrots and roast for two minutes. Spread the vegetables in a baking tray. Arrange the marinated chicken with the marinade on the vegetables.

2 Cook in the oven till done. Meanwhile, for the glaze, mix orange juice, red chilli flakes, honey and mustard paste and cook in a non-stick pan till reduced to half the original quantity. Mid-way through the baking, glaze the chicken with this mixture and continue to bake till the chicken is cooked. Serve hot.

Non-Veg | Preparation 60 mins | Cooking 30 mins | Serves 4 people

Main Course - Seafood, Chicken And Mutton

Chutney Chicken

INGREDIENTS

450 grams boneless chicken, cut into 1-inch cubes

2 teaspoons cumin seeds

2 teaspoons coriander seeds

5-6 black peppercorns

2-3 cloves

4 tablespoons fresh coriander leaves

2 tablespoons fresh mint leaves

½ inch ginger

8-10 cloves garlic

2-3 green chillies

1 cup skimmed milk yogurt, drained

Salt to taste

1 teaspoon *garam masala* powder

1 lemon, cut into wedges

1 Dry roast cumin seeds, coriander seeds, peppercorns and cloves. Cool slightly and grind along with coriander leaves, mint leaves, ginger, garlic and green chillies to a fine paste.

2 In a bowl, mix yogurt, salt and *garam masala* powder with the ground paste and marinate the chicken pieces in this mixture for an hour, preferably in a refrigerator.

3 Heat a non-stick pan, add the marinated chicken, cover and cook, stirring now and then, till the chicken is cooked and the gravy has thickened.

4 Serve hot with lemon wedges.

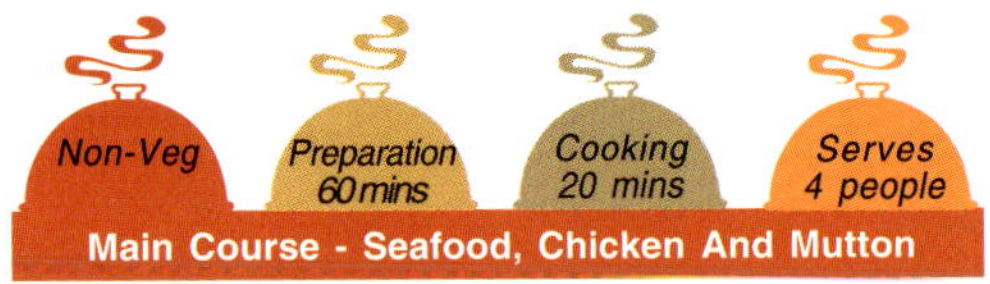

Baked *Mince*

INGREDIENTS

2 cups chicken mince (400 grams)

5-6 garlic cloves, chopped

2 medium onions, chopped

1 medium carrot, chopped

1 celery stalk, chopped

½ cup Chicken Stock (*page 92*)

1½ teaspoons Worcestershire sauce

Salt to taste

7-8 black peppercorns, crushed

½ cup tomato purée

2-3 sprigs fresh parsley

¼ teaspoon black pepper powder

A pinch of nutmeg powder

9 tablespoons skimmed milk

4-5 medium potatoes, boiled and mashed

1. In a non-stick frying pan, roast chicken mince, garlic and onion on low heat for two to three minutes. Add carrot and celery. Stir and add chicken stock. Cover and simmer till the mince is cooked.
2. Stir in Worcestershire sauce, salt, crushed peppercorns and tomato purée and cook for another minute. Preheat the oven to 200°C/400°F/Gas Mark 6. Chop parsley, reserving one sprig for garnishing.
3. Add salt, black pepper powder, chopped parsley, nutmeg powder and milk to mashed potatoes and mix well. Put the mixture into a piping bag with a star nozzle.
4. Spread the prepared mince in a glass baking dish. Pipe the mashed potatoes on top in rosettes. Bake in the oven for ten to twelve minutes or till the potatoes turn golden. Serve hot, garnished with the reserved sprig of parsley.

Saag *Gosht*

INGREDIENTS

3 medium bunches (350 grams each) spinach

600 grams boneless lamb/mutton, cut into 1½-inch cubes

¾ cup skimmed milk yogurt

1 tablespoon ginger-garlic paste

½ teaspoon turmeric powder

2 teaspoons red chilli powder

½ teaspoon coriander powder

1 teaspoon *garam masala* powder

Salt to taste

3-4 green chillies

2 bay leaves

3 green cardamoms

1 black cardamom

6 cloves

1 inch cinnamon

6-8 black peppercorns

1 Mix together half a cup of yogurt, ginger-garlic paste, turmeric powder, one teaspoon of red chilli powder, the coriander powder, *garam masala* powder and salt to taste. Marinate the lamb cubes in this mixture for about half an hour.

2 Blanch spinach in boiling salted water for one minute. Drain and refresh in cold water. Grind spinach and green chillies together to a coarse paste. Set aside.

3 Heat a thick-bottomed pan. Add bay leaves, green cardamoms, black cardamom, cloves, cinnamon, peppercorns, cumin seeds and roast till they emit a fragrant aroma. Add garlic and roast till it turns light brown. Add onions and cook till translucent.

4 Add half the ginger strips, remaining red chilli powder and marinated lamb cubes. Cook on high heat, stirring continuously for two minutes. Add remaining yogurt

1 teaspoon cumin seeds

6-8 garlic cloves, chopped

3 medium onions, sliced

1 inch ginger, cut into thin strips

½ tablespoon dill leaves (*suva*), chopped

1 teaspoon dried fenugreek leaves (*kasoori methi*), roasted and crushed

and one cup of water and bring to a boil. Transfer the mixture into a pressure cooker and cook till the cooker gives out eight whistles.

5 Wait till the pressure reduces. Open the lid, add spinach paste, dill leaves and salt if necessary. Cook till lamb is tender and well-coated with spinach.

6 Sprinkle *kasoori methi* and serve hot, garnished with remaining ginger strips.

Non-Veg | Preparation 30 mins | Cooking 30 mins | Serves 4 people

Spaghetti with Mixed Vegetables *and Herb Sauce*

INGREDIENTS

250 grams wholewheat spaghetti

1 medium carrot, cut into 1-inch cubes

1 small head broccoli, separated into small florets

8-10 fresh button mushrooms, halved

1 medium green capsicum, cut into 1-inch pieces

½ teaspoon mixed herbs, roasted

3 tablespoons wholewheat flour (*atta*)

1½ cups skimmed milk

Salt to taste

¼ teaspoon white pepper powder

1 tablespoon fresh parsley, chopped

1 Boil the spaghetti in five cups of water till just done. Drain, refresh in cold water and set aside. Blanch carrot and broccoli separately in one cup of boiling water for two to three minutes. Drain and refresh in cold water. For the herb sauce, lightly roast wholewheat flour in a non-stick pan. Add milk and whisk rapidly so that no lumps form. Strain if required. Add salt, pepper and mixed herbs. Mix and set aside.

2 In a non-stick pan, add the carrot, broccoli, mushrooms, capsicum and spaghetti, toss well and cook on moderate heat for two minutes. Add the herb sauce and mix well. Adjust seasonings. Serve, garnished with chopped parsley.

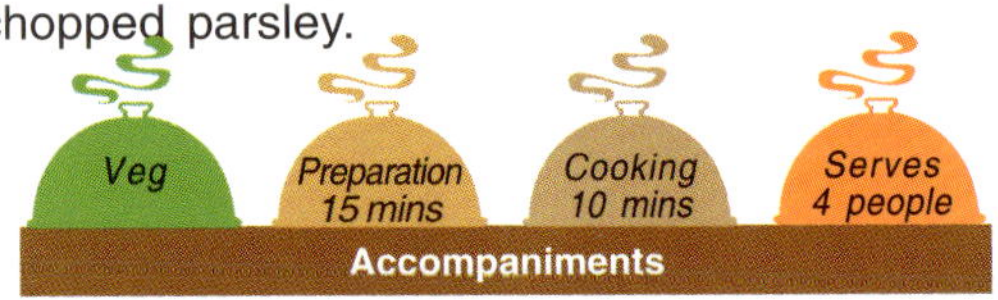

Beetroot *Raita*

INGREDIENTS

1 small beetroot

2 cups skimmed milk yogurt, whisked

1 teaspoon roasted cumin powder

½ teaspoon red chilli powder

1 tablespoon fresh coriander leaves, finely chopped

Salt to taste

1 Boil, peel and grate beetroot. Chill in the refrigerator.

2 Add roasted cumin powder, red chilli powder, fresh coriander leaves and salt to the yogurt and mix well.

3 Add chilled beetroot and mix gently.

4 Serve chilled.

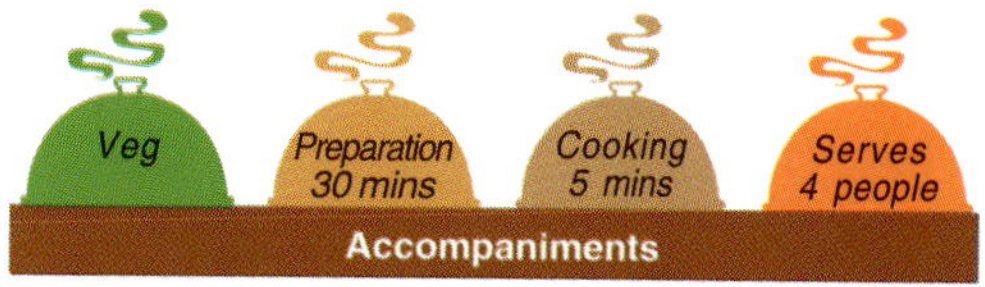

Brown Rice Vegetable Pilaf

INGREDIENTS

1½ cups brown rice

2 medium carrots, cut into ½-inch cubes

10-12 French beans, cut into ½-inch pieces

¼ medium cauliflower, separated into small florets

6-7 medium fresh button mushrooms (optional), halved

½ cup green peas, shelled

1 bay leaf

2-3 cloves

1 teaspoon cumin seeds

1 inch cinnamon

2 green chillies, slit

Salt to taste

2 tablespoons fresh coriander leaves, finely chopped

Note: *Brown rice is available at health food stores.*

1. Soak brown rice in four to five cups of water for two hours. Drain and set aside.

2. Heat a deep non-stick pan, add bay leaf, cloves, cumin seeds and cinnamon and roast for a few seconds or till fragrant. Add drained rice and roast for one to two minutes more. Add four cups of water and bring to a boil.

3. Add carrots, French beans, cauliflower, mushrooms and green chillies. Stir and bring to a boil. Add salt and mix. Lower heat, cover and cook till almost done.

4. Add green peas and mix gently. Cover and cook till done. Serve hot, garnished with fresh coriander leaves.

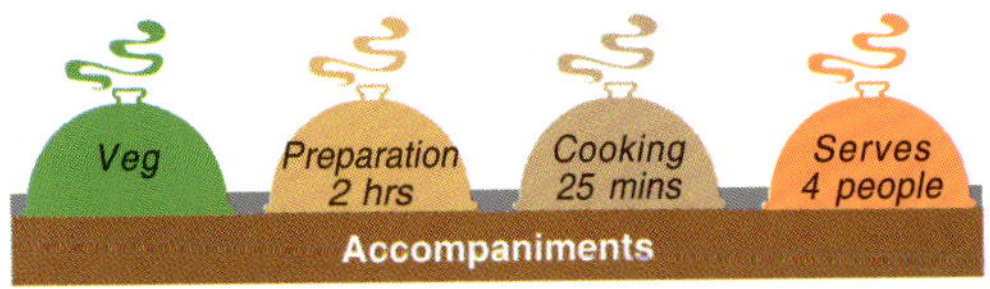

Chicken *Kofta Pulao*

INGREDIENTS

250 grams chicken mince
1½ cups Basmati rice
4-5 green cardamoms
1 bay leaf
7-8 cloves
Salt to taste
4 tablespoons fresh coriander leaves, finely chopped
1 inch ginger, finely chopped
1½ teaspoons red chilli powder
20 black peppercorns, crushed
½ teaspoon green cardamom powder
2 medium onions, finely chopped
3 medium tomatoes, finely chopped
1 teaspoon coriander powder
½ teaspoon cumin powder
½ teaspoon *garam masala* powder

1 Soak rice in four to five cups of water for fifteen to twenty minutes. Drain and set aside.

2 Boil six cups of water in a deep pan with green cardamoms, bay leaf, cloves and salt for about five minutes. Strain and set aside.

3 Take chicken mince in a bowl and add two tablespoons of coriander leaves, ginger, half the red chilli powder and crushed peppercorns, and the green cardamom powder. Add salt to taste. Mix well and make marble-sized *koftas*.

4 Boil the *koftas* in the flavoured water till cooked. Drain and set aside. Reserve the cooking liquid.

5 Heat a deep non-stick pan and roast onions till translucent. Add chopped tomatoes, remaining red

chilli powder and crushed peppercorns, coriander powder and cumin powder. Add salt and sauté till tomatoes are cooked.

6 Add drained rice and cook for two to three minutes. Add three cups of reserved cooking liquid and one cup of water. Bring to a boil, cover tightly with a lid and simmer for ten minutes.

7 Uncover the pan, add the cooked chicken *koftas* and mix gently. Cover and cook for two to three minutes.

8 Sprinkle *garam masala* powder and the remaining coriander leaves. Serve hot with a *raita* of your choice.

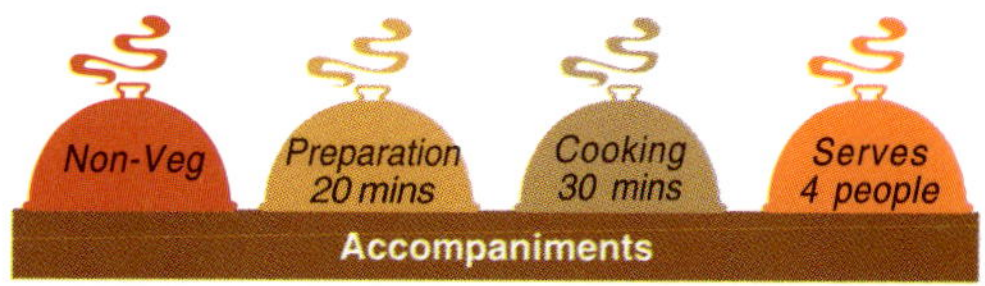

Masaledar *Dal*

INGREDIENTS

½ cup split pigeon peas (*toovar/arhar dal*)

Salt to taste

¼ teaspoon turmeric powder

2-3 green chillies, slit

1 teaspoon cumin seeds

3-4 whole dried red chillies

A pinch of asafoetida

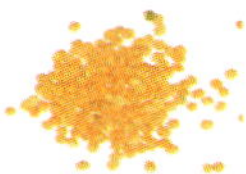

2 medium onions, chopped

½ teaspoon red chilli powder

1 teaspoon coriander powder

2 medium tomatoes, chopped

½ teaspoon *garam masala* powder

2 teaspoons lemon juice

2 tablespoons fresh coriander leaves, chopped

1. Soak *dal* in four cups of water for half an hour. Drain and pressure cook with two cups of water, salt, turmeric powder and green chillies till done.

2. Heat a deep non-stick pan. Roast cumin seeds, whole red chillies, asafoetida and onions for two to three minutes.

3. Add red chilli powder, coriander powder and tomatoes and cook further for five minutes on moderate heat.

4. Add cooked *dal* and mix well. Add *garam masala* powder, more salt if necessary and simmer for five to ten minutes.

5. Add lemon juice and coriander leaves and stir to mix. Serve hot with steamed rice.

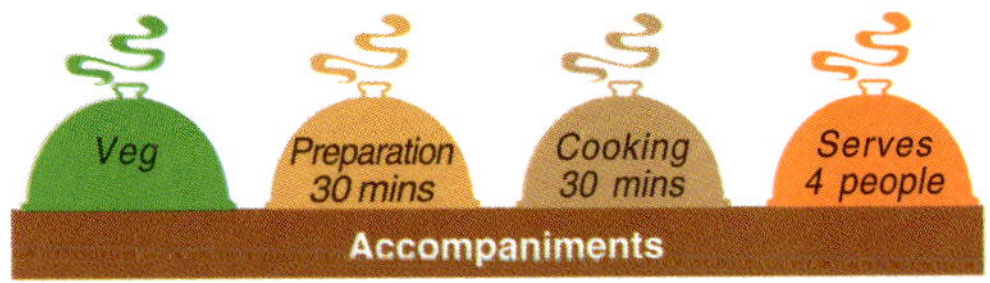

Roasted Capsicum and Tomato *Dip*

INGREDIENTS

1 medium red capsicum, seeded and quartered

5 medium tomatoes, seeded and quartered

5-6 garlic cloves, finely chopped

Salt to taste

2 teaspoons sugar

2 tablespoons lemon juice

1 sprig fresh parsley

1 Preheat oven to 180⁰C/350⁰F/Gas Mark 4.

2 Arrange red capsicum and tomato together with garlic on a baking tray. Sprinkle with salt. Bake for twenty to twenty-five minutes and allow to cool. When cool, peel capsicum and tomato wedges and chop.

5 Heat a non-stick pan and roast garlic for a minute. Add capsicum and tomatoes and cook for two minutes. Add more salt, if necessary and the sugar. Mix well. Cook for another two minutes and add lemon juice. Mix again. Serve, garnished with a sprig of parsley.

INGREDIENTS

250 grams penne
5 medium tomatoes
6 garlic cloves, crushed
2 medium onions, sliced
1 teaspoon crushed red chillies
1 tablespoon oregano
Salt to taste
5-6 basil leaves

Penne *Arrabbiata*

1. Blanch tomatoes, peel, remove seeds and chop coarsely.
2. Cook penne in plenty of salted boiling water, drain, refresh in cold water and set aside.
3. Heat a non-stick pan, add garlic and roast until light brown.
4. Add onions, roast until transluscent and then add crushed red chillies, oregano and tomatoes.
5. Cook for about five minutes on low heat. Add salt and mix well.
6. Add penne and roughly torn basil leaves and toss lightly. Serve hot.

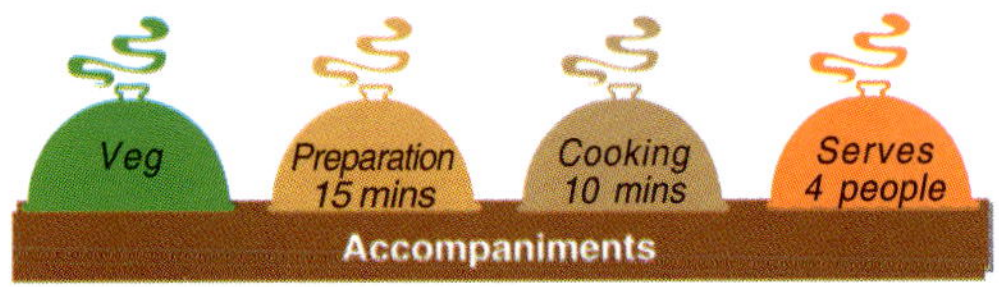

Palak and Chhena Parantha

INGREDIENTS

2 cups wholewheat flour (*atta*) + extra for dusting

1 medium bunch spinach, (350 grams) chopped

100 grams skimmed milk cottage cheese (*chhena/paneer*)

½ cup skimmed milk yogurt, whisked + to serve

1 small onion, finely chopped

½ teaspoon carom seeds (*ajwain*)

2 tablespoons fresh coriander leaves, chopped

2 tablespoons fresh mint leaves

2 green chillies, chopped

½ teaspoon cumin powder

1 teaspoon *chaat masala*

1 teaspoon *garam masala* powder

Salt to taste

1 Place wholewheat flour in a deep bowl.

2 Add remaining ingredients and knead into a medium soft dough with sufficient water. Cover and rest the dough for fifteen minutes.

3 Divide the dough into twelve equal portions and shape into balls.

4 Roll out into thick *paranthas*. Heat a *tawa* and roast *paranthas* on moderate heat on both sides till brown and crisp.

5 Serve hot with skimmed milk yogurt.

Date and Tamarind Chutney

INGREDIENTS

15-20 dates (*khajur*)

1 cup tamarind pulp

2 teaspoons cumin seeds

¼ teaspoon fennel seeds (*saunf*)

½ cup jaggery, grated

2 teaspoons red chilli powder

1 teaspoon dried ginger powder (*soonth*)

1 teaspoon black salt

Salt to taste

1 Wash dates, stone and chop roughly. Dry roast cumin seeds and fennel seeds. Cool slightly and grind to a powder.

2 Mix together dates, tamarind pulp, cumin and fennel powder, jaggery, red chilli powder, dried ginger powder, black salt, salt and four cups of water.

3 Cook on moderate heat till the mixture comes to a boil, lower heat and simmer for six to eight minutes, or till the *chutney* is thick.

4 Cool and serve, or store for later use.

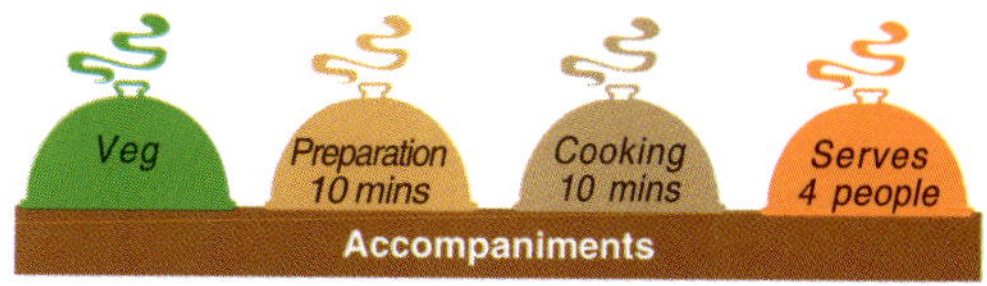

INGREDIENTS

1½ cups Basmati rice

1 cup chickpeas (*Kabuli chana*)

2 tablespoons tea leaves

Salt to taste

1½ cups skimmed milk yogurt

1 teaspoon ginger paste

1 inch ginger, cut into thin strips

½ cup fresh mint leaves

1 teaspoon green chilli paste

1 teaspoon red chilli powder

1 teaspoon turmeric powder

Chholay Biryani

1. Soak *kabuli chana* overnight or for six hours in four cups of water. Drain and pressure cook in four cups of fresh water with salt and tea leaves tied in a piece of muslin, till tender. Remove the muslin cloth bag and drain chickpeas.

2. Marinate boiled chickpeas in yogurt, ginger paste, ginger strips, half the mint leaves, green chilli paste, red chilli powder, turmeric powder, *garam masala* powder and garlic paste.

3. Soak rice in three cups of water for about half an hour. Drain. Boil four cups of water in a deep pan with salt, green cardamoms, bay leaves and cloves. Add rice and cook till half done. Drain.

4. Dissolve saffron in warm milk and mix in *kewra* water.

1 teaspoon *garam masala* powder

1 teaspoon garlic paste

5-6 green cardamoms

2-3 bay leaves

2-3 cloves

A few strands of saffron

1 tablespoon skimmed milk

A few drops of *kewra* water

¼ cup fresh coriander leaves, chopped

Chef s Tip: *You can use chholay masala to add more flavour to this biryani.*

5 Place the marinated chickpeas in a deep non-stick pan.

6 Spread cooked rice over the chickpeas evenly. Sprinkle dissolved saffron and half the coriander leaves over the rice.

7 Cover the pan tightly and cook on low heat for fifteen minutes or till rice is done.

8 Serve hot, garnished with remaining coriander and mint leaves.

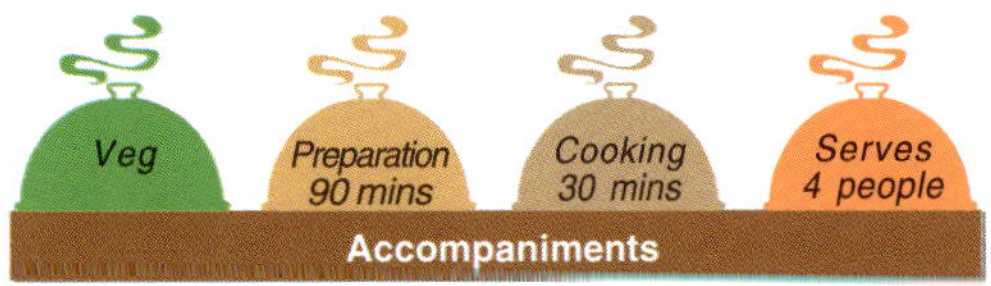

Palak *Raita*

INGREDIENTS

2 medium bunches (350 grams each) spinach

1 green chilli

2 cups skimmed milk yogurt

Black salt to taste

1 teaspoon roasted cumin powder

Salt to taste

1 Blanch one bunch of spinach in boiling water, drain and refresh in cold water. Drain, squeeze out excess water and purée with one green chilli in a blender. Shred the remaining spinach.

2 Whisk yogurt and add spinach purée, black salt and roasted cumin powder. Mix well and chill in the refrigerator.

3 Heat a non-stick pan. Add shredded spinach and cook over high heat for three to four minutes, stirring continuously.

4 Season with salt and mix well. Continue to cook on high heat till the spinach is almost dry. Take the pan off the heat and cool.

5 Mix the spinach with the flavoured yogurt just before serving. Adjust salt and serve chilled.

Green Mango and Onion *Chutney*

INGREDIENTS

3 medium green, unripe mangoes, peeled, stoned and chopped

2 medium onions, grated

4-6 green chillies, chopped

1 tablespoon pomegranate seeds (*anardana*)

2 tablespoons lemon juice

½ teaspoon black salt

Salt to taste

½ teaspoon sugar

1. Put the green mangoes, green chillies, pomegranate seeds, lemon juice, black salt, salt and sugar into a blender and blend till smooth.
2. Adjust the consistency by adding water.
3. Squeeze the grated onion to remove excess juice and add to the *chutney*.

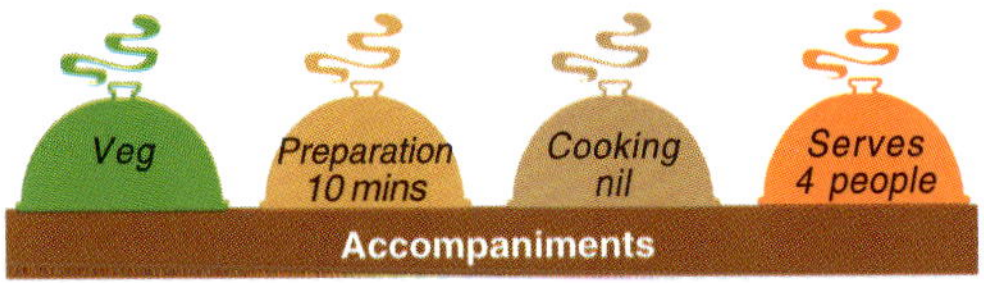

Tamatar *Ki Kadhi*

INGREDIENTS

12 small tomatoes, puréed

4 teaspoons gram flour (*besan*)

½ teaspoon turmeric powder

1 teaspoon red chilli powder

Salt to taste

1 teaspoon sugar

½ teaspoon mustard seeds

A pinch of asafoetida

½ teaspoon cumin seeds

5-6 curry leaves

4-5 whole dried red chillies

2 tablespoons fresh coriander leaves, chopped

1 Mix tomato purée, gram flour, turmeric powder, red chilli powder, salt and sugar. Whisk till well blended. Stir in two cups of water.

2 Heat a deep non-stick pan and roast mustard seeds, asafoetida, cumin seeds, curry leaves and whole red chillies till fragrant.

3 Add the tomato mixture and bring to a boil. Reduce heat and simmer for ten minutes.

4 Serve hot, garnished with coriander leaves.

Veg | Preparation 15 mins | Cooking 15 mins | Serves 4 people

Accompaniments

Dhania Pudina *Parantha*

INGREDIENTS

2 cups wholewheat flour (*atta*)

¼ cup fresh coriander leaves, chopped

¼ cup fresh mint leaves, chopped

Salt to taste

2 teaspoons *chaat masala*

½ cup skimmed milk yogurt

1 Place the wholewheat flour and salt in a bowl. Add coriander leaves, mint leaves and enough water to make a soft dough. Cover and rest the dough for twenty to twenty-five minutes. Divide the dough into eight equal portions and shape into balls.

2 Mix yogurt and *chaat masala*. Roll out each ball into a medium-sized *chapati*. Spread a tablespoon of the yogurt mixture. Fold the *chapati* like a fan and twist it back into the form of a ball. Set aside for five minutes.

3 Roll out each portion into a *parantha* of five to seven inches diameter. Cook on a hot non-stick *tawa* till both sides are a light golden brown. Before serving, crush the *paranthas* lightly between your palms to open out the layers.

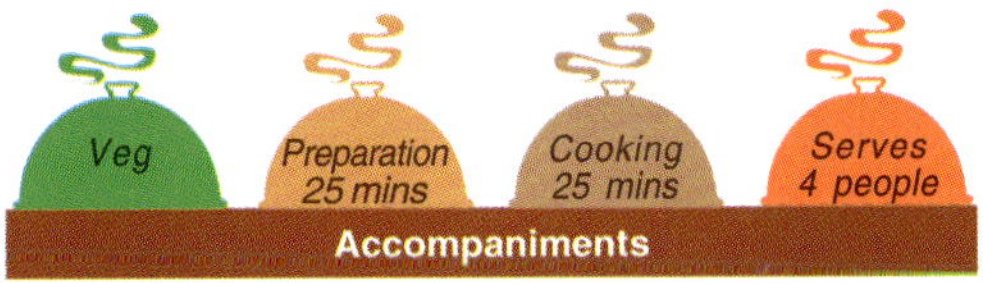

Pineapple Yogurt *Fool*

INGREDIENTS

½ medium fresh pineapple, cut into small cubes

½ cup sugar

1 inch cinnamon

½ cup drained skimmed milk yogurt

1 Mix pineapple, sugar and cinnamon in a pan and stew for thirty minutes. Set aside to cool.

2 Remove pineapple pieces and mix with drained yogurt. Process together in a blender. Chill in the refrigerator.

3 Serve chilled.

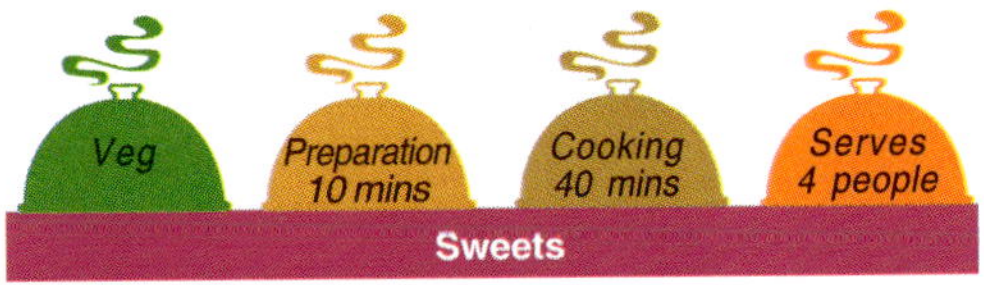

INGREDIENTS

6 tablespoons vermicelli (*sevian*)

10-15 strands saffron

1½ litres (7½ cups) skimmed milk

8 tablespoons sugar

20 raisins (*kishmish*)

1 teaspoon green cardamom powder

1 tablespoon almond slivers, toasted

Zafrani *Sevian*

1 Heat a non-stick pan and roast vermicelli on moderate heat till lightly browned.

2 Pour milk into a deep pan and bring to a boil. Lower heat and simmer till reduced to half the quantity.

3 Add sugar and cook till it dissolves. Add vermicelli and raisins and cook for two minutes.

4 Take the pan off the heat. Add saffron and green cardamom powder and stir well.

5 Serve hot or cold, decorated with toasted almond slivers.

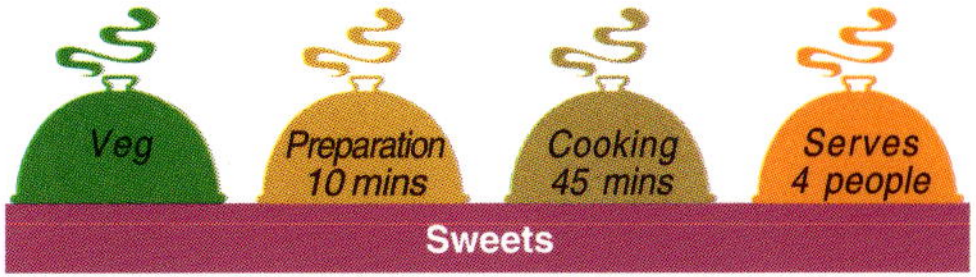

Sitaphal Basoondi

INGREDIENTS

1½ litres (7½ cups) skimmed milk

1 cup custard apple *(sitaphal)* pulp

½ cup sugar

½ teaspoon green cardamom powder

10-12 pistachios, sliced

1 tablespoon *charoli* (*chironjee*)

10-12 almonds, blanched and slivered

3-4 rose petals (optional)

1 Bring the milk to a boil in a heavy bottomed pan on high heat. Lower heat and simmer for half an hour. Keep stirring so that the milk does not burn and stick to the bottom of the pan. When the milk reduces to half the original quantity, add sugar. Simmer for five more minutes. Take the pan off the heat and set aside to cool.

2 When cool, add custard apple, green cardamom powder, sliced pistachios and *charoli*.

3 Transfer to a serving bowl and garnish with almond slivers and rose petals.

4 Serve cold.

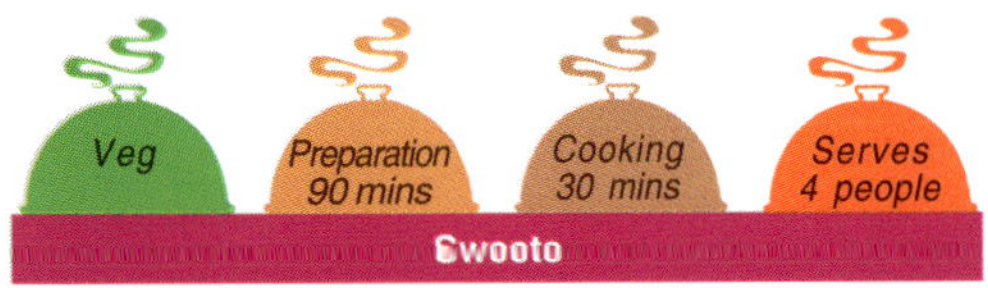

Gajar Ki Kheer

INGREDIENTS

2 medium carrots, grated

1 litre (5 cups) skimmed milk

$^{1}/_{3}$ cup sugar

¼ teaspoon green cardamom powder

2 tablespoons raisins (*kishmish*)

1 Bring the milk to a boil, reduce heat and simmer till it is reduced to three-fourth its original volume.

2 Add carrots and cook on low heat for about fifteen to twenty minutes or till the carrots are completely cooked.

3 Add sugar and cook, stirring occasionally, till sugar dissolves.

4 Add green cardamom powder and stir well.

5 Serve garnished with raisins.

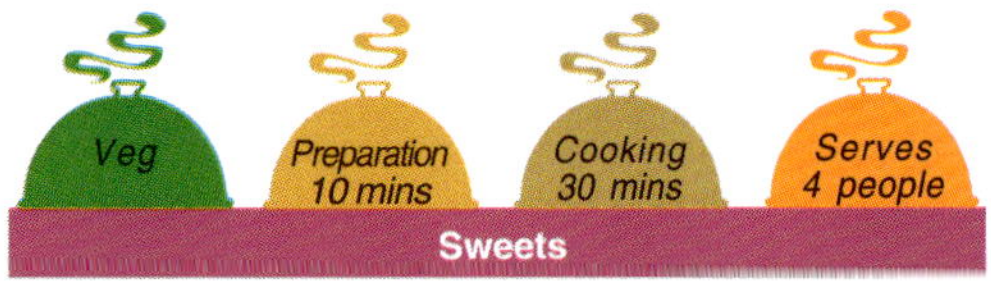

Chhanar *Payesh*

INGREDIENTS

½ cup *chhena (paneer)*, made from skimmed cow's milk

1 litre (5 cups) skimmed milk

½ cup sugar

5-6 almonds, blanched and chopped

7-8 pistachios, blanched and chopped

Chef s Tip: *If cow's milk chhena is not available use chhena made from buffalo's milk. I recommend chhena made from cow's milk because it is low in fat.*

1. Boil milk, lower heat and simmer till reduced to half the original quantity.
2. Add sugar and cook till it dissolves.
3. Mash *chhena* in a bowl. Add it to the milk. Simmer for two minutes.
4. Sprinkle chopped nuts and serve cold.

Anjeer *Ka Meetha*

INGREDIENTS

250 grams dried figs (*anjeer*)

250 grams dried, seedless dates

¼ cup skimmed milk powder

4-5 almonds, roasted and slivered

1 Soak figs in three cups of water for three to four hours. Boil them in the same water in which they were soaked, for three to five minutes.

2 Take the pan off the heat, drain the figs and cool slightly. Reserve some figs and purée the rest. Chop the reserved figs.

3 Chop dates roughly and soak in two cups of hot water for fifteen to twenty minutes. Drain and purée.

4 Mix the two purée and add skimmed milk powder. Mix well and cook on low heat for fifteen to twenty minutes or till well blended. Add the chopped figs and simmer for another two to three minutes. Serve garnished with almond slivers.

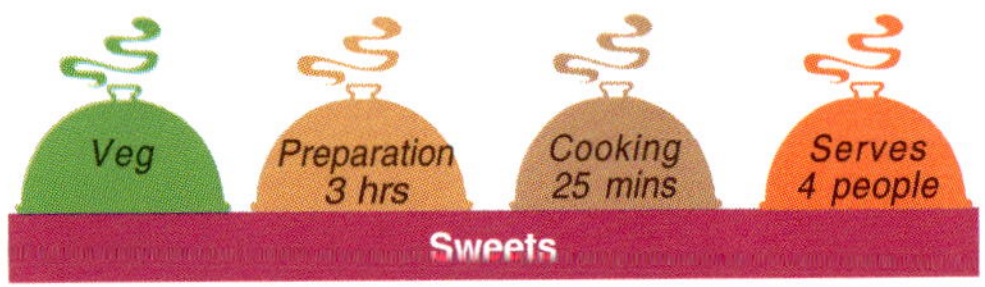

Annexure

Chicken Stock

Boil 200 grams chicken bones in water for 5 minutes. Drain and discard water. Boil blanched bones with a roughly chopped carrot, celery stalk, leek, 2-3 parsley stalks, 6-7 black peppercorns, 5-6 cloves, 1 bay leaf and 10 cups of water. Remove any scum which rises to the surface and replace it with more cold water. Simmer for at least one hour. Remove from heat, strain, cool and store in a refrigerator till further use.

Goda Masala

Roast 1 cup coriander seeds, 2 tablespoons cumin seeds, ¼ cup stone flower 6 two-inch sticks cinnamon, 16 green cardamoms, 25 cloves, ¾ teaspoon caraway seeds, 15-18 black peppercorns, 10-12 bay leaves, 1 teaspoon nagkeshar, 2 blades mace, 3 tablespoons grated dried coconut, 1 teaspoon sesame seeds, 3 whole dried red chillies and 1 teaspoon asafoetida one by one in a little oil. Cool and grind to a fine powder. Makes 100 grams of *goda masala* powder.

Vegetable Stock

Peel, wash and chop 1 onion, ½ medium carrot, 2-3 inch celery stalk and 2-3 garlic cloves. Place in a pan with 1 bay leaf, 5-6 peppercorns, 2-3 cloves and 5 cups of water and bring to a boil. Lower heat and simmer for 15 minutes and strain. Cool and store in a refrigerator till further use.

From Our Nutritionists' Desk

The purpose of giving you these oil-free recipes is to bring some newness to your daily diet. We live in a world that is moving at breakneck speed. And in this stressed style of living, more and more people face the problem of raised cholesterol levels. And if this is not scary enough, we have life-style diseases like obesity, diabetes and hypertension. Hence the pressing needs to decrease the intake of oil and fats.

The Need of the Hour

It would be perfectly correct to say that high cholesterol levels are also a result of a lack of exercise and regard for good health. Lack of time causes neglect of things that matter: like looking after oneself, following a healthy eating pattern and also incorporating an exercise schedule into one's daily routine. Now is the time to tighten our belts simply because more and more young people seem to be suffering from all sorts of life-style diseases that shorten life spans. This book presents a gentle guideline for eating low-fat food, which is made without the addition of seed extracted oil.

Learn to Switch

Many people wonder about the pros and cons of an oil-free diet. The important fact to remember is that we cannot do without oil. But we can certainly do with less oil in our food.

And the sooner we adopt a fat-free mode of cooking the better for our health in the long run. One weak moment of hunger that made you demolish a samosa adds a whopping 369 calories to your day's intake. Or have a small 105 grams pack of your favourite French fries, which will add 360 calories. Instead, two idlis will provide only 60 calories and be just as filling. Small things make a difference: switching over from buffalo's milk to cow's milk saves up to 50 calories and 2.4 gms of fat per 100 gms. The time has come to make your choices.

It is not really an Oil-Free World

You will realize while browsing through the book that we have not used any visible oil in the recipes. One can easily be led to think that an oil-free world exists. But it does not. The fact is, all foods contain some trace of oil fat like poppy seeds, coriander seeds, cumin seeds, cloves, peppercorns, sesame seeds and turmeric powder do have some fat content. These ingredients have been used in almost all the recipes ensuring that they are not misjudged as being 'fat free'. They are `low fat' and there are no great health hazards in having low fat foods. For those who are concerned it would be interesting to know that a hundred grams of poppy seeds contain 19.3 grams of fat. Similarly, cashew nuts, groundnuts, dried coconut, fresh coconut, almonds and walnuts also have considerable amounts of fat. Well, even arhar/toovar dal has a fat content - 100 grams has 1.5 grams of fat as compared to 3.7 in a moong dal preparation. Dals are not eaten raw and once they are cooked they do have additions of seeds and spices.

We Do Need Oil

Our bodily functions operate at the optimum when they are lubricated well and for all this all naturally present oils are good. We are all aware that oil adds taste and an appetizing appearance to anything you make. Yes, even some salads taste better with a dash of salad oil or olive oil. Oil is an integral part of most recipes because it removes the unpalatability of the dish and adds the needed softness, flavour and nutrients.

Some reasons why we need fat:

- Fat is a concentrated source of energy and is essential for the absorption of fat soluble vitamins.
- It is an important constituent of cells and helps in growth and development.
- Fat consists of Essential Fatty Acids (EFA). A no-fat diet deprives the body of these EFA and it could lead to growth retardation, skin lesions and liver degeneration. Dryness and scaliness of skin have also been observed.
- EFA are so named because they cannot be processed or manufactured by the body. They play an important role in growth, reproduction, skin and hair conditions and healing of wounds. They also play a structural role in cell membranes.

Weight loss and no-fat go together. But a long term no-fat diet is undesirable as it can lead to some serious problems like :

- Dry, itchy and scaling skin
- Dry, dull and and dandruff-ridden hair
- Poor healing of wounds
- Neurological disease
- Heart disease (arteriosclerosis)
- Skin diseases
- Degenerative conditions such as cataract, arthritis and cancer.

It is better to follow a diet that is low in fat but healthy in essential proteins, carbohydrates, vitamins and minerals. A good diet is primarily what we should be looking at. Hence this book of recipes that have been made without oil. If you have binged one day, the following day or two try making use of the recipes in this book.

And remember…
Eat sensibly, exercise and have a long and healthy life!